CARE AND COMPASSION

EMPATHY FOR OTHERS

RACHAEL MORLOCK

PowerKiDS press

NEW YORK

Published in 2020 by The Rosen Publishing Group, Inc.
29 East 21st Street, New York, NY 10010

Editor: Rachel Gintner
Designer: Michael Flynn

Photo Credits: Cover JGI/Jamie Grill/Blend Images/Getty Images; cover, pp. 1, 3–4, 6, 8, 10–12, 14–16, 18–20, 22–24 (background) TairA/Shutterstock.com; p. 5 leezsnow/E+/Getty Images; p. 7 Michael Rougier/The LIFE Picture Collection/Getty Images; p. 9 PIXOLOGICSTUDIO/Science Photo Library/Getty Images; p. 10 Holly Kuchera/Shutterstock.com; p. 11 pixelheadphoto digitalskillet/Shutterstock.com; p. 13 Tom Wang/Shutterstock.com; p. 14 wavebreakmedia/Shutterstock.com; p. 15 Monkey Business Images/Shutterstock.com; p. 17 Ian Walton/Getty Images; p. 18 Bernard Weil/Toronto Star/Getty Images; p. 19 Rubberball/Nicole Hill/Getty Images; p. 21 Catalin Petolea/Shutterstock.com; p. 22 sirtravelalot/Shutterstock.com.

Cataloging-in-Publication Data

Names: Morlock, Rachael.
Title: Care and compassion: empathy for others / Rachael Morlock.
Description: New York : PowerKids Press, 2020. | Series: Spotlight on social and emotional learning | Includes glossary and index.
Identifiers: ISBN 9781725301986 (pbk.) | ISBN 9781725302013 (library bound) | ISBN 9781725301993 (6pack)
Subjects: LCSH: Empathy--Juvenile literature. | Empathy in children--Juvenile literature.
Classification: LCC BF723.E67 M67 2020 | DDC 152.4'1--dc23

Manufactured in the United States of America

CPSIA Compliance Information: Batch #CSPK19. For further information contact Rosen Publishing, New York, New York at 1-800-237-9932.

CONTENTS

WHAT'S EMPATHY? 4

THINKING AND FEELING 6

HOW IT WORKS 8

STRONGER TOGETHER 10

RECOGNIZING EMOTIONS 12

LISTEN UP! 14

SHOWING COMPASSION 16

SEEDS OF CHANGE 18

THE POWER OF IMAGINATION 20

EMPATHY IN ACTION 22

GLOSSARY 23

INDEX 24

PRIMARY SOURCE LIST 24

WEBSITES 24

CHAPTER ONE

WHAT'S EMPATHY?

Do you ever cry when you see a sad movie? If your friend tells you excitedly about their new bike, do you feel happy? Have you had an argument with a brother or sister and tried to understand their point of view? If these situations sound familiar, then you probably practice empathy every day without realizing it! Empathy happens when you notice and imagine what other people are thinking, feeling, and experiencing.

Empathy is similar to sympathy. When you are sympathetic, you care about someone and hope they'll feel better. Empathy also involves caring, but it brings you closer to others than sympathy can. When you practice empathy, you not only pay attention to what others are experiencing, you also share their emotions and **perspective**. Empathy is a powerful way to connect with others and show them you care.

With empathy, you experience the emotions and perspectives of others almost as if they're your own. When a friend is sad, you feel sad, too.

CHAPTER TWO

THINKING AND FEELING

Empathy can be broken down into two parts—thinking and feeling. You need both parts of empathy to understand the full experience of others.

Feeling with others often happens like a **reflex**. When you see a friend crying, you may feel tears stinging your eyes, too. If a classmate giggles, you might feel happy and laugh without knowing the joke! You can often share strong emotions with others without understanding what led to them.

Sometimes, though, you have to think more about others to share their feelings. You can think about the way they look and what they say to find clues about their emotions. You can also imagine their situation. How would you feel in their shoes? The more information you have or can imagine about someone, the more likely you are to share and understand their feelings.

Psychologist Carl Rogers believed that empathy could help people heal and grow, especially in **therapy**. Rogers practiced empathy by listening carefully and trying to understand the emotions of others.

CHAPTER THREE

HOW IT WORKS

Empathy starts inside you. The human body is made up of cells, and the cells in the brain and **nervous system** are called neurons. These special cells use chemicals to send messages about what's happening in and around you. For example, when you eat ice cream, neurons in a certain part of your brain send you messages about the experience. Some scientists are studying how special neurons may send certain messages when you watch someone else eating ice cream, even if you aren't eating it yourself.

Some scientists think these mirror neurons may be the building blocks of empathy. They may allow your brain to imagine the experiences, actions, and **sensations** of people around you. We often copy others and learn by watching them. These connections, which scientists think might be **automatically** made in your brain, are just the beginning. Empathy also involves a purposeful effort to understand others.

There are about 86 billion neurons (possibly even more!) that send messages inside your brain. Whether you're watching or performing an action, there's activity in your brain that people can study.

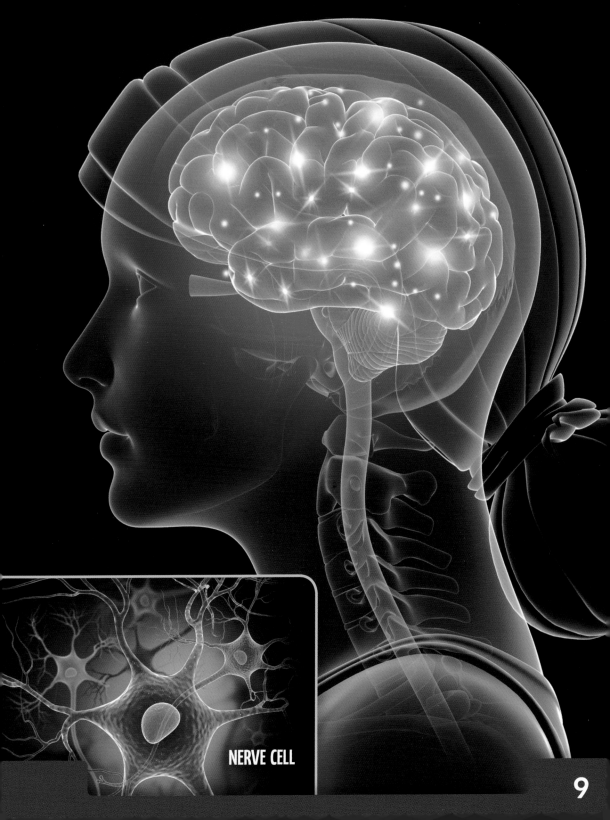

NERVE CELL

CHAPTER FOUR

STRONGER TOGETHER

Ever since the earliest humans, empathy has helped people connect with each other. It's likely that animals, including **primates**, dogs, and rats, also experience empathy. These **species** have all gained empathy over time. They've used it as a tool for raising their young and working together as a team for survival. The natural role of empathy shows how important social relationships are for humans and other animals.

When you're sad or scared, doesn't it help to feel understood by loved ones? Being able to give and receive empathy helps you form close, healthy relationships with others.

Empathy strengthens families. If you think about the bond between a parent and their child, you can see empathy at work. Empathy allows parents to care for their children. When babies cry, their parents use empathy to understand their feelings, comfort them, and provide what they need.

Friendships and communities also grow stronger with empathy. It helps people more easily share their experiences and emotions with each other. Then community members can **cooperate** as they work toward common goals.

CHAPTER FIVE

RECOGNIZING EMOTIONS

A large part of practicing empathy is identifying emotions in others. In addition to your words, your face, body, and voice can tell others how you feel. Even if you don't think about it, your facial muscles usually move into certain positions based on your emotions. You smile when you're happy, pout when you're sad, or frown when you're angry. Facial **expressions** provide information about emotions that others can recognize.

Body language also points out emotions. Body language includes movements or positions that reflect your feelings. Another strong clue is your voice. For example, your voice might sound high when you're excited or quiet and low when you're sad. Learning about emotions can help you recognize them in yourself and others. When you look for the emotions behind different facial expressions, types of body language, and tones of voice, you take a step toward empathy.

Can you identify these facial expressions? Now make the same faces in front of a mirror. Can you imagine how the woman feels? What could make her feel that way?

CHAPTER SIX

LISTEN UP!

You don't have to rely only on expressions or body language to understand emotions. You can also use words. The more you practice talking about feelings, the easier it is to share them with others. There are hundreds of words to describe your emotions. It's a good idea to build up a rich language of emotions so you can label the way you and others feel.

Active listeners show they care by working hard to understand. They don't interrupt or rush. They're generous with their time and attention.

Listening to others is a powerful tool for understanding their feelings. You can practice active listening by making eye contact, paying attention, asking questions, and repeating what you hear to make sure you understand. You can make guesses about how someone is feeling, but you might not always guess right! Make sure you're open to hearing what others have to say. Then you can give them the space they need to express their true feelings.

CHAPTER SEVEN

SHOWING COMPASSION

There are many ways you can **respond** to other people's emotions once you understand them. When you show sympathy, you feel sorry for others. When you experience empathy, you feel their emotions with them. When you show compassion, you are moved by your feelings to help others. Compassion is the next step after empathy. You understand what others feel, and you take action to help them. Compassion comes in many different forms, depending on the problem you're trying to help with.

A bullying situation can provide an example of empathy in action. Many students feel sorry for the person being bullied. Others imagine or remember the pain of being bullied. When a student stands up for their bullied classmate, they turn their empathy into compassion. They act on their understanding of how another is feeling in order to make things better.

In the 2016 Olympics, rival runners Abbey D'Agostino and Nikki Hamblin crashed into each other and fell. They showed empathy and compassion by helping each other finish the race.

CHAPTER EIGHT

SEEDS OF CHANGE

Empathy helps you make connections. Usually, those connections bring your family members, friends, classmates, or neighbors closer together. Other times, empathy creates connections with people you'll never meet. You can empathize with people who look, sound, and act differently from you and live in faraway places. You don't have to be the same as someone to understand how they feel. People around the world share emotions, needs, and hopes that unite them, and empathy can bring them together.

When Craig Kielburger (shown here at age 13) was 12 years old, he read about a 12-year-old former slave in Pakistan named Iqbal Masih. Kielburger's empathy with Masih inspired him to create an organization to fight child labor.

When empathy becomes compassion, it leads to big and small changes in the world. Something as simple as inviting a new classmate to eat at your lunch table can have a big effect on that one person. Compassionate acts can also start great changes that affect many people. They begin with imagining what it's like to be someone else.

CHAPTER NINE

THE POWER OF IMAGINATION

Experiencing and showing empathy isn't always easy, but everyone can get better with practice. Reading books, watching movies, looking at art, and listening to music are good ways to practice. Good storytelling helps you imagine what it's like to be someone else. When you pay attention to characters in stories, you see life from their point of view.

You can also use your imagination to understand people around you. If your neighbor seems grumpy, you might wonder what happened to make him upset. If your sister is angry that you borrowed her markers without asking, try to imagine why she feels that way. Ask yourself questions about the people you meet.

Imagination is the key to empathy. It helps you see from someone else's perspective. It can also be the key to compassion. How can you make the world a better place?

Books can help you see life through someone else's eyes. Just like the characters you read about, everyone you meet has their own story of emotions and experiences.

CHAPTER TEN

EMPATHY IN ACTION

A scramble of thoughts, feelings, and experiences lies behind every action you take. The first step toward empathy is recognizing the way your own thoughts and feelings work and the way your experiences affect you. This helps you understand and imagine the thoughts and feelings of others.

When you show empathy, you tell others that you care about them. You care enough to try to see life from their perspective. You listen to the story they tell in order to understand it, not to judge it. You accept their feelings and look for ways to help.

It's important to both give and receive empathy in your relationships. Practicing empathy this way creates close and healthy connections with others. It can also lead to acts of compassion that are powerful enough to affect the people, relationships, and world around you.

GLOSSARY

automatically (aw-tuh-MAA-tihk-lee) Happening without thought, or happening immediately.

cooperate (koh-AH-puhr-ayt) To act or work with others to a common end.

expression (ik-SPREH-shuhn) The look on someone's face.

nervous system (NUHR-vuhs SIS-tuhm) The system of nerves that sends messages for controlling feeling and movement between the brain and body.

perspective (puhr-SPEK-tiv) Point of view.

primate (PRY-mayt) The group of animals that includes monkeys, gorillas, and humans.

psychologist (sy-KAH-luh-jist) A person who studies psychology, or the science or study of the mind and behavior.

reflex (REE-fleks) An action that happens without thought.

respond (ruh-SPAHND) To do something as a reaction to something that has happened or been done.

sensation (sen-SAY-shuhn) An awareness or feeling involving one of the five senses.

species (SPEE-sheez) A group of plants or animals that are all the same kind.

therapy (THAYR-uh-pee) Talking with another person to figure out one's feelings.

INDEX

A
active listening, 15
animals, 10

B
body language, 12, 14
brain, 8
bullying, 16

D
D'Agostino, Abbey, 16

E
emotions, 4, 6, 11, 12, 14, 16, 18, 20
expressions, 12, 14

G
goals, 11

H
Hamblin, Nikki, 16

I
imagination, 20

K
Kielburger, Craig, 18

N
nervous system, 8

P
perspective, 4, 20, 22

psychologist, 6

R
reflex, 6
relationships, 10, 11, 22
Rogers, Carl, 6

S
sympathy, 4, 16

T
therapy, 6

V
voice, 12

W
words, 12, 14

PRIMARY SOURCE LIST

Page 7
Dr. Carl Rogers. Photograph. Michael Rougier. January 1, 1966. The LIFE Picture Collection and Getty Images.

Page 17
Abbey D'Agostino and Nikki Hamblin at the 11th day of the 2016 Olympics. Photograph. Ian Walton. August 16, 2016. Getty Images Sport.

Page 18
Craig Kielburger, Canadian child labor activist. Photograph. Bernard Well. November 21, 1996. *Toronto Star*.

WEBSITES

Due to the changing nature of Internet links, PowerKids Press has developed an online list of websites related to the subject of this book. This site is updated regularly. Please use this link to access the list: www.powerkidslinks.com/SSEL/care